Where's That Insect?

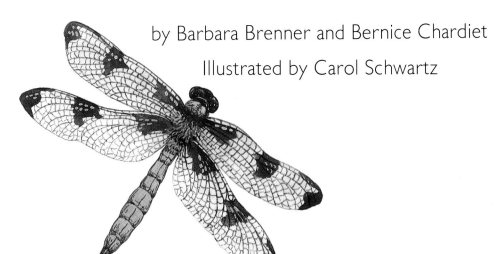

by Barbara Brenner and Bernice Chardiet

Illustrated by Carol Schwartz

Cartwheel
·B·O·O·K·S·™

SCHOLASTIC INC.

Text copyright © 1993 by Chardiet Unlimited, Inc.
Illustrations copyright © 1993 by Carol Schwartz.
All rights reserved. Published by Scholastic Inc.
CARTWHEEL BOOKS is a trademark of Scholastic Inc.
HIDE & SEEK SCIENCE is a trademark of
Daniel Weiss Associates, Inc.

Library of Congress Cataloging-in-Publication Data
Brenner, Barbara.
Hide and seek science : where's that insect? / by Barbara Brenner
and Bernice Chardiet ; illustrated by Carol Schwartz.
p.   cm.
Summary: Presents information about different kinds of insects.
The reader is invited to find insects hidden in the illustrations.
ISBN 0-590-45210-X
1. Insects—Juvenile literature.   2. Picture puzzles—Juvenile
literature.   [1. Insects—Miscellanea.   2. Picture puzzles.]
I. Chardiet, Bernice.   II. Schwartz, Carol, 1954-   ill.
III. Title.
QL467.2.B74   1993
595.7—dc20   92-20906
                                                                  CIP
                                                                   AC
12 11 10 9 8 7 6 5 4 3 2 1   3 4 5 6 7 8/9
Printed in Malaysia
First Scholastic printing, March 1993

Introduction

Some of them fly,
Some of them crawl,
Some of them swim—
And that's not all....

Some of them hop,
Some of them sting,
Some of them buzz,
Some of them sing.

Come see them all
In this book.
All you have to do
Is look, look, look!

Come to the Leafcutter Ant Parade!

It's easy to see how the leafcutter
ants got their name.
They are also known as parasol ants.
This one has been out all morning cutting
leaves.
Can you find her in the parade?
A tiny guard ant is riding on the leaf.
Even though it's so small, the guard ant
will fight if enemy ants attack.

It's a Fact:
When the leafcutters get home to their
nest, worker ants will chew the leaves into
a green paste. They'll mix the paste with
mushroom spores. Tiny mushrooms will
grow, and the ants will have food.

Which Is Which?

These are monarch butterflies.
One is a male.
One is a female.
They are almost exactly alike, so look
very carefully. The male monarch has a
black spot on each wing.
Now look at the big picture.
See if you can find two male monarchs on
the "butterfly tree."

MALE

FEMALE

It's a Fact:
Monarch butterflies go south in the fall.
They travel as many as 2,000 miles
together every year. They gather on
favorite "butterfly trees" to rest until the
winter is over. Each year new groups of
monarchs fly south. They follow the
same route. And they stop to rest on the
very same trees!

A Dragonfly Hunt

You'll often find dragonflies near ponds, where they help people by eating huge numbers of mosquitoes.
Can you find this dragonfly on the log?

He's with dragonflies of other colors. But he doesn't pay any attention to them. He's on the lookout for a mate—one of his own species, who looks just like him. Since there are 450 different kinds of dragonflies, his search seems doomed. Or is it? A dragonfly exactly like him is nearby.
He will find her. Can you?

It's a Fact:
The dragonfly's ancestors were around at the time of the dinosaurs. They had wings two feet across!
Dragonflies are probably the best flyers in the insect world. They can fly up to 35 miles an hour and stop in the blink of an eye.

Honeybee Business!

The honeybee on this page
is gathering nectar to take to the hive for
making honey. The queen bee is the
biggest honeybee in the hive.
Can you find her in this picture?

It's a Fact:
The queen bee is the *only* bee in the hive that lays eggs. She may lay as many as 2,000 eggs *a day*. That's all she does. Worker bees take care of the eggs and feed the queen.

A Little Cricket Music

Here is a tree cricket resting on a blade of
grass.
Her pale green color and jointed legs
blend in with the grass and weeds.
Can you find the tree cricket in the
picture?
Who else do you know here?
A honeybee and a monarch butterfly!

It's a Fact:
Male crickets chirp to attract a mate by
clasping their forewings over their backs
and rubbing them together. They chirp
faster when it's warm and slower when
it's cold. In fact, you can tell how cold it
is outside by counting a cricket's chirps.
Count how many chirps the cricket makes
in 15 seconds. Then add 39. That's the
temperature!

Ladybug, Ladybug, Don't Fly Away

The ladybug is sometimes called a ladybird or a lady beetle.
Scientists often know what kind of ladybug they're looking at by the number of spots it has.
Ladybugs can have as few as two or as many as twenty-two spots.
Can you find this five-spot ladybug in the big picture?

It's a Fact:
Ladybugs help people by eating many harmful insects.
Sometimes farmers buy ladybugs and put them on their plants. By the way, not all ladybugs are ladies. Males are called ladybugs, too.

Tiny Pests, Big Trouble

They're tiny green bugs no bigger than
the head of a pin.
But aphids cause plenty of trouble!
They suck the life out of plants.
Look at this row of corn in the farmer's
field. One of the ears is being attacked
by aphids. How many aphids can you
find on that corn plant?
Who's there to eat the aphids?

It's a Fact:
Aphids are the world's greatest pests.
Luckily they have enemies like the
ladybug. But they also have friends like
the dairy ant. Dairy ants love to lick the
sticky honeydew that aphids produce. A
dairy ant will even squeeze or stroke an
aphid to get more honeydew out of it.

Flying Lights!

In the daytime, this firefly looks like any
small bug. But on a summer night, fireflies
really shine!
It's a lovely sight.
Uh-oh. Danger!
Toads are the fireflies' enemies.
And there's one lurking under a leaf!
Let's hope that firefly sees the toad.
Can you see the firefly?
Can you find the toad?

It's a Fact:
A firefly is not a fly. It's a beetle. And its
light doesn't come from fire. It comes
from a chemical in its body. Firefly light
can be greenish, yellowish, or reddish. The
fireflies that give off the brightest light
live in South America.

Water Bug Monsters!

Can you believe it?
Two giant water bugs are hiding on the
bottom of this pond!
One is carrying the eggs of his babies on
his back. The other is his mate.
She stuck the eggs to his shell with a
special "glue" from her body.
Can you find the water bug monsters?
Do you also see a snail and a school of
baby bass?

It's a Fact:
The giant water bug is among the largest
of the bugs—about 2½ inches long.
Usually it sits on the bottom of a quiet
pond, waiting for a small fish or a frog to
come along. Then, *zap!* The giant water
bug grabs it and shoots poison into it.
The poison turns the frog or fish to liquid.
Then the big bug drinks its dinner! After
a giant water bug finishes its meal, all
that's left of its victim is a hollow skin.

Now You See 'Em, Now You Don't!

These are sphinx moths.
They fly around at night and rest on trees during the day. Their colors make them look like part of the tree.
There are three sphinx moths hiding in the big picture.
Can you find them?

It's a Fact:
All moths are born from eggs and spend time as caterpillars before they become moths. After they become moths, the males look for mates. A male moth can pick up the scent of a female from a mile away.

Did You Ever See a Stick Walking?

This insect is called a walking stick. Can you see why?
When it walks on a tree, you'd never know it was there.
Can you find the walking stick in the big picture?

It's a Fact:
Walking sticks come in several colors, and they seem to pick trees to match! Green walking sticks are often found on the green leaves of trees. Brown ones rest on the bark of brown trees.

A Garden Party

This is a yellowjacket wasp.
Below it is a honeybee.
They look a lot alike, don't they?
No wonder. They're relatives.
But they usually don't hang around
together.
Nevertheless, this garden seems to be full
of yellowjackets and honeybees.
How many yellowjackets can you find?
How many honeybees are there?

It's a Fact:
Some wasps and honeybees live in large
groups. Yellowjackets make paper nests
out of chewed-up wood. Honeybees make
hives. They both have queens. And they
both have stingers, so don't get too close!

More Insects Who Hide...

Here are a few shy caterpillars that don't
want you to find them.
You'll have to look very hard.
They hide by looking like other things.
Find a caterpillar that looks like the edge
of a leaf. Find one that looks like part of
a tree. Find one that looks like the leaves
of a plant. Find one that looks like the
flowers it is resting on.

It's a Fact:
Caterpillars turn into other insects. Some
become moths. Others become butterflies.
This change is called metamorphosis.

The Great Insect Round-Up!
Hail! Hail! The gang's all here!
How many do you know?

Aphid
less than ⅛″

Caterpillar
Various sizes, depending on species

Cricket
¾″

Dragonfly
1¾″ to about 2⅝″

Firefly
7/16″

Giant Water Bug
2½″

Honeybee
Queen: about 1″

Honeybee
Worker: ½″

Ladybug
less than ¼″

Leafcutter Ant
Small worker: 1/10″
Other workers: ½″

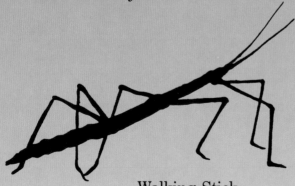

Monarch Butterfly
3½″ to nearly 4″

Sphinx Moth
½″ to about 5″ (depending on species)

Walking Stick
2¾″

Yellowjacket Wasp
13/16″